Light Thickens

Light Thickens

Poems by

Elizabeth Biller Chapman

The Ashland Poetry Press
Ashland University
Ashland, Ohio 44805

Printed in the United States of America

Paperback ISBN: 978-0-912592-66-4

Library of Congress Catalog Card Number: 2008941474

Cover Art by Matt Phillips, *Painter/Poet with Red Line*, 1992
Collage monotype, 30 x 22 in.
Collection of the de Saisset Museum, Santa Clara University
Gift of the artist 2002.8

Book cover design by Mike Ruhe

Ohio Arts Council
A STATE AGENCY
THAT SUPPORTS PUBLIC
PROGRAMS IN THE ARTS

Grateful acknowledgment is made to the following publications, in which these poems, some in earlier versions, have appeared.

Bellevue Literary Review, "Lunch at My Late Mother's, Improvised," "The Old Man Washes His Boat, Ballycotton"
Blueline, "A Cup of Cold Water," "Vespers for Phoebe," "Detail, Snow in the Countryside"
Image, "Elements of January"
Manzanita Quarterly, "Ballymaloe, This Time of Year," "Tropicbirds"
North American Review, "At Caroni Swamp"
Poetry, "Light Thickens," "On the Screened Porch"
Prairie Schooner, "And the Crow Makes Wing to the Rooky Wood," "Quinces"
Sand Hill Review, "Grout," "Tilth," "Stake," "In This at Last May Sun, the House"
Santa Clara Review, "Breakfast with Persephone," "Winter's Empire"
South Dakota Review, "On Chesterman Beach"
The Texas Observer, "The Nesting Turtle at Matura Beach, Trinidad"
Tiferet, "Motet for the Guttering World"
Water-Stone Review, "December Psalm"
The Writer, "Brief Visit"

Further acknowledgments can be found on page 73.

For Francis Murphy,
with affection and gratitude

Contents

On Chesterman Beach/1

The Figs Ghostly on Their Branch

Tilth/5
Light Thickens/6
Grout/8
The Breakfast Fruit/9
Crazy Walk/10
The Old Man Washes His Boat, Ballycotton/13

And the Crow Makes Wing to the Rooky Wood

And the Crow Makes Wing to the Rooky Wood/17
On the Screened Porch/18
Brief Visit/19
Winter's Empire/21
Ballymaloe, This Time of Year/23
Ladder to My Room/24
Lunch at My Late Mother's, Improvised/25
December Psalm/26

Our Fragile House, Filling with Your Names

Quinces/29
Daughter/31
Elegy/32
Breakfast with Persephone/34
For My Daughter Seven Weeks Married/35
Wainscott, Like As the Waves/36

Tatters of Aphrodite

Tropicbirds/39
In Asa Wright's Garden/40
A Cup of Cold Water/41
The Nesting Turtle at Matura Beach, Trinidad/42
Caroni Swamp/43
Now spring is reaching toward you again/45

I Call Her My Jungle Gardenia

Perseid/49
Hydrangeas/50
I Call Her My Jungle Gardenia/51
To a Deer in the Forest/52
Knitting/53

Fish Hook of Summer Stars

Vespers for Phoebe/57
That Nickering/58
Elements of January/59
Detail, Snow in the Countryside/62
For Someone Lost/63
Motet for the Guttering World/64
Nocturnal, 12 Adar/65
Stake/66
Memory of Stanley Kunitz, Northampton/67

Epilogue
In This at Last May Sun, the House/69

Notes/70
Further Acknowledgments/73

On Chesterman Beach

Non semper erit aestas
It will not always be summer
—Hesiod

What is the word for the calling of bald eagles
leaving now for their dark interior rivers,
their song, spiraled downward—low, gurgled,
sweeter than you'd think, for raptors—is an ancient flute.
Walking this foreshore in a slant sun
I cannot keep a straight line: the kelp, heaping
feather-boa, sea-palm; long stipes pulled up by the tide
and dropped here, turning brown; the edge of old age.
Everything falling. Everything awash with mid-September.
Ceaseless, that sound of waters brings me to dream
                              the ancient names—
Clayoquot, Wickanninish, Ucluelet—hearing them as waves
                              bearing me north
to Kitimat, where First Nations trade spring *oolichan*,
that clear oil saved for fry-bread. Winter food.
We owe a lot to the moon: intertidal
bivalve and mollusc; this rucked-up skirt of sand;
razor clams lie in the cold, creamed honey of their shells.
On this coast of complex inlets and coves
it's hard to know direction.
Still, westering, I make my fall collage: Sitka cone and bark,
pearlescent scatter of salt,
one barnacle's white house, its lonely presence, like a skull.

The Figs Ghostly on Their Branch

Tilth

November's rake, rasping over difficult ground—
it's mounded where we buried our old cat—

two handfuls of ash in a cedar box.
Sometimes I wake at night, hoping she's not cold there,

as if I'd heard my father's long-ago raking.

His mother, dead in the great flu,
left when he was ten, how could he bear that?

His voice, a fragile canopy; the yellowed fig tree's
falling, piecemeal: *Leave something fresh behind.*

Bluebells and the common snowdrop—white cloud
on sharp blue sky, in spring—will drift loose.

My green trowel's clumped with clay. I sprinkle food
and fill this corner where the earth slopes down.

Light Thickens

Intimacies of grooming: his girth already loose,
   my chaps stripped off, I stand in straw, undo
   the throat-lash; noseband. Paddock smell
                            of horse and grain.
"Por favor, Francisco,"
   handing me a sponge, he unwraps the chestnut's legs
              and, I do not
understand this—the growing dark, the healing of bone,
   the life of the barn and the life behind the barn,
                       chickens flapping,
   a groom cleaning his car at the wash-rack—all this,
                    taking over, he asks
"Isabel. Ha visto la pelicula, *El Norte?*"
   "Si. Tan triste, pero beautiful."
"Es verdad. En mi grupo. . . there were eighty, crossing.
There was a *coyote.*"
              "Scary." "Scary." We both say it, tears
in our eyes. "Buena noche,"
       "Buena noche."

Moonlight on the antique sled; the figs ghostly
                      on their branch.
I have had trouble sleeping this year:
   my husband's walking dwindled to a few steps;
   lurches from the bed; tacking like a toddler holding on
across the house.
             The loss of myelin. Some falls.
At those times, raw, he's a crustacean without its shell.

We have our rituals. Daily, for months now,
   two aged animals receive essential fluids. My husband
   the good physician ever, prepares the bag and drip-set.

Lactated Ringer's, hung from a kitchen nail
   while I as nurse make sure the field is ready:
   an old quilt, once on my daughter's bed, folded

on the clothes dryer.
                              A handwash, he unsheathes a clean
                                      eighteen-gauge needle,
and we dialyze: First cat, 150 milliliters. Same again, second cat.
    For one more day
    they lie stretched on our green doormat in the morning sun.

There's no explaining
    attachment, although the curious inquire, nor how
    by being loved, we're lovable—it isn't
possible, it simply happens, that silence we fly to
                                      like birds
in summer, bathing in the garden, the fresh day—
    Run your hand over my forehead, love.
                              You are my haven.

Grout

is what holds everything together: the one-by-one
hexagonal tile,
a more secure footing for your weakening legs. With the left
      foot, step
and drag the right.
Step, drag; step, drag. Shuffling, after eight years, the best they can.
We are cranky here.
We have chosen this chaos: Last Thursday, the worst day, all
      the screens
and the power off,
the tips of my shoulder blades crawled upward. Scared. I will never
make a good wife. "God,"
says my confessor, "understands your situation perfectly." *Who telleth
the number of the stars
and calleth them all by their names.* The Big Dipper's handle points
      straight
down. What does that mean?
You dream rarely now, but this cold spring night
elliptical metaphors
pop right out of the pattern: April is untrustworthy. We have agreed
on cobalt blue;
the curbless shower, its drain angled downward. A workman stays
      overtime.
His mortar's gray
and gritty. That tile floor looks just like the ocean.

The Breakfast Fruit

This morning a slow air climbed out of night—
stillness, then bird song at the edges where
wintering, the mistle-thrushes feed
on big black ivy berries. A barrow scraped
and dogs' feet scuffled on the stones.
                                    We lay waking
hip against hip sunk into exhausted sleep
after our journey. The wheelchair's getting
prodded, a brake-cable snapped.
Then, as beech and ash logs smoldered, an old tune
plucked on the mandolin untethered us.
                                    Today's the first
Sunday of Lent: eggs large as their slotted spoon,
brown bread whose yeast has risen on dark treacle,
warmed to blood heat. And in this white bowl
on a blue checked cloth—prunes and whole peeled apricots,
poached in a simple syrup with golden raisins,
                                    fresh bananas sliced on top.

Two ducks, paired, fly over the field in front.
Spring makes her overture. There is still love left.

Crazy Walk

I.

As if
     spilled from some giant Mason jar, the redwood seeds
     scatter over our deck, where the ramp begins. Each one,
a round black fleck of summer;
the tree, the sower, rusted now and grown
too close against a neighbor's house, unhealthy.

My husband has put on his Panama hat
and strapped his right leg to the footrest.
Unplugged, soundless, his chair eases past
           "the isthmus"—cat bowls, mail table—
and the door we've had to widen.

He's still
     a handsome man, the long slim shape and large head
like a Victorian apostle-spoon.

I fetch one cat, then the other.

When the tortoise-shell drapes
     willingly across his green cargo pants
When her calico sister stops
     yelping and is settled, kneading her towel
     in the Jazzy's wire basket
When he's steered around that curve
              by the driveway
bees in lavender—
         we relax a little.

Nearly five, on this warm late afternoon
    . . .and in the evening withhold not thy hand,
The Lockhinch buddleia exhales her medium blue
honey of July.

II.

Circling toward sundown
                wheeling and by foot
beside the green tangle of creek—
Marlowe, Lytton, Palo Alto Avenues,
our peaceable kingdom—
          coming back. . .

The little girl
          thin, in her shorts and top,
swinging (the tree trunk padded with a pillow tied on)
hops down to get a better look
                at the four of us
                male female; human feline; fur, all
launched an hour ago, an ark upon the waters
if you think of this daylily light
                    as a wave.

Braking, with just the right amount
of gravity, my husband tells her
                "A family outing, but now
                the cats are tired. They're twenty."
(Frisky's tail, drooped down between his calves.)
"I read a story once," she pauses, "about an old man. . ."

Held in that child's gaze for a second,
our day like a wide circle of lawn
          or a swath of linen as yet unstained,
I am gripped with fear, and look away
          reminded how people ask
                    "If you had known. . ."
          I was there at the spinal tap, and I chose.

                But she's already continuing
"who had no one to cuddle, or cuddle him, so
he adopted a kitty just like <u>that</u>,"
pointing at Tabby, whose scrabbling in her rumble-seat
                bespeaks her dodgy bladder.

"So I want to know
is she soft?" "Very soft."
          for thou knowest not whether shall prosper this or that.
Moving in, berry-shaped, the clouds of summer signify—
                    we wave—it's time to go.

The Old Man Washes His Boat, Ballycotton

This bay—where long ago my friend caught
a basking shark with just a line, no rod—
with its long green water and the nesting cliffs
of spring: We will look back on this day, hilled
like the cantle of a saddle, the street
mysteriously named The Cow, where
a yellow Lab puppy sniffed our hamper
holding smoked salmon and ham. We pushed
the chair (my husband's blue baseball cap
and soft sweater worn at the elbows) down that
grassed path, a single table at the edge—
small kee-yawing of choughs and hawthorn's white
billowing seas in the hedgerow
shielding us from wind that once had blown
a lovesick lady who would row her skiff
across the strait to her beloved
keeper of the light.
       Now as we ate
he nibbled on a sandwich, sipped his soup,
politely waiting for the chocolate we'd set in the shade.
"No complaints," despite the apparatus invading,
and weakness of breath. There was a red dory
opposite amid the Queen Ann's lace, its black keel
showing. Gannets rode the breeze, watched
an old man bring his bucket full of sea
up along the pier, then slosh and scrub, debarnacle
the bottom. He made many trips,
not noticing my clamber on the stone shingle;
the five bleached cockle shells I picked.
My husband's upper lids, lowered. The old man
plies his trade, his wages earned: a clean boat.
Is labor prayer? Our arms around each other
and the noonday tide, brightening and dimming.

And the Crow Makes Wing
to the Rooky Wood

And the Crow Makes Wing to the Rooky Wood

Wings of moss, the fabric of this place where
lambs toward evening chew upon their damp green
grasses till each ewe's distinctive call, then
butt under the belly to nurse. Mother—
a sparrow hurls his dawn song at our wall.
Those droplet fingers I nuzzled, your linen
shroud, all becoming mossed—only for an
hour or so at a time can I feel whole.
What thrift, this tide incoming among lined
limpets whose pale blue circles are left behind.
A sand like honeycomb: presence and absence
from me. . . *and she moved through the fair.* Listen—
will you hear field blackbirds, the way they dance,
tap with their feet, pretending they are rain.

On the Screened Porch

Suppertime. Corn, cooked—some milk
in the water—always threatens to boil over. You let those ears
stand, when it's seethed, two minutes. More tender that way.
My mother and I

at summer's edge, the garden not as it was, but
lush, intensely green, the lawn's near perfect.
She says, "I love the shadows long"—

> Roof angle, oak trunk, golden chain, extending
> that moment a tree-clinging bird
> creeps along one branch's underside, gleaning the bark—

No need for light overhead, to see
the cloth's rosy pattern,

a familiar mild clicking of cubes: as a child
I was proud to carry in my father's iced coffee and pour,
from the Russel Wright jug, his dollop: the cream
  descending

in meanders, like memory
downward, the liquid's dark bitterness gone.

Brief Visit

Snow as a shawl
wraps my mother's house the way I remember

in the night plows scraped
a newspaper man has made

the only footprint
Early before anyone

my shovel's dry squeak through powder
back porch to front door

the window box frozen silent
slumbering on

Indoors an old barometer is tapped
is rising We sift and reminisce

four apples cored for baking everywinter's smell
melting sugar and cinnamon

The oilburner man
has come with his tank and hose Once

when the streetcar didn't run
my father's spade and galoshes bricked an igloo

whose high walls opened to the sky
Colors here are primary

eggsalad at midday and yellow
in their vase tulips who like their feet cold

my mother's red woolen shirt
two cardinals poking through a hedge

Time eddies from the roof
in a white whirl

Winter's Empire

Outside the world congeals
                    though it is morning
sitting by the bed I say my name
              taking her hand
which infection has fevered
      Do you know where you are Mrs. B.? *Home*
      Home Dr Ellenbogen echoes Now lift up your
      arms Higher And she does
      eyelids barely able to squint I'm making you NPO
      Nihil per os
Bag after bag waits to enter and travel
to that lower right lobe Strong medicine tagged red

*

From the Riesman Building 12th floor I see
children's tracks on a schoolyard's recent snow

Her speech indistinct
                   I want that sense back
like the claret scarf dropped on the jetway rushing here

I've loved you longest known you
              My whole life
Even a little longer she says pulling to her lips

my hand as if the flaw or sudden gust of wind
that veered the candle from its beeswax core
            had turned to vapor
      Could you hand me the nasal cannula please?
      on her long shift the young doctor in this house
      called Clement is asking Where is your pain?
      ruling out biliary duct gallstone sludge
all radiating from the weakened lung
             Mother could you sleep?

Jan. 19th *The Boston Globe* reports bird sightings
hooded mergansers off Nantucket and in Mt. Auburn Cemetery
                               a single screech owl
the previous day Hold on Mother I'm coming In the night
she'd thought I was already there bending over

singing as she used to Brahms' lullaby
and goodnight with roses bedight and lilies bedecked
over baby's sweet head Lay thee
                             down now and rest
Raising her chin a smidgen she is humming.

Ballymaloe, This Time of Year

"You'll be wanting the lambs." Too late. Tatters of mother wool
caught on the wire, the sheep turned out graze
imperturbable as paving stones, high up the gorse-stitched hill.

You have learnt something. That means, you have lost something.

The Irish playwright knew a north wind. Cold, dry, the weather's
cleared a place in me, somewhere between a meadow and a cave,
this room across the courtyard (instep of the house, its Norman
        keep).

Sparrows are building on the creviced wall, rooks in the beeches.
From the lengthening peal which is spring, can I separate
one bell, its quick work, its dodging, its slow work?

The sky's gray-pink, midmorning, a Cork cockle-shell.
Walking by the stream, I saw an otter in plain view—
compact and purposeful—bound along the grassy verge,

not looking cold, in fact, not cold (the thick brown fur),
another's tail, scuttling. Proof of a pair, a holt
safe in the bank-side; fish; frogs. Near Cloyne

the water lives. And I drank the lesser celandine's
gold yolk, drank the sticky green of horse chestnut buds
each one a chalice. As for the otter's deep unknown intention,

he simply shows himself, the way a love-debt gets repaid.

Ladder to My Room

If at times snow, decanted, would sift in
and I'd waken to a drift on the sill
(a broad seat, where I watched the cherry trees

doubling their pink, caught more than once by a late spring
storm—then like torn moths), it would know a girl's
chenille spread, those thin white tufts mocking snow;

the cherrywood bookcase with small cut out
hearts I've just given away to Margaret,
quietest of my mother's carers. Her grieving

face lit up, seeing it propped between the window
and the dun-colored chair (primal
as the horse whose black stripe runs from mane to tail).

Dun inside me the day she died, that wild
telling, over and over, "We're all here," her closed eyes
turning toward the voice I tried to keep steady.

The Amherst poet rhymed Death with Earth:
"Putting Love away we shall not want"
I'm smelling the Schraffts chocolate box,

too many books, old woollens. A memory of bread:
those soft Parker House rolls I'd sneak upstairs
to nibble in moments of difference.

Yesterday it snowed—October—and the cold
drove the workmen away, Declan and Paddy, whose ladder
was left leaning against the house; no screens.

As the last, long daylight's climbing down,
a strand of air turns rose. Clear twilight, now.
I hear the children's footfalls leave the park.

Lunch at My Late Mother's, Improvised

We've been tasting dust: closet, drawer,
an attic fan roused, not much help, and grumbling.
Those gray and white plates of every day,
and the party bowls, packed and shipped.
My sisters having gone, another round is over.
        Everything I chose was chipped.

      Clinging to the same thread, five of us here—
old friends, her housekeeper, my first-born, grown—
find unexpired tuna, cucumber, light
and dark swirl pumpernickel bread.
We set a table in the open air.
        No one's right in that corner

      opposite the 40's bassinet like an airy cage on legs
where she sat once—white high heels,
a sleeveless and striped summer dress. Now
knifed cantaloupe, a chocolate cake perhaps not quite
defrosted. I struggle with the ice trays.
        "These chairs'll last forever,"

      Mr. Butts said, brooming the garage. Some long-
forgotten daylilies stretch across the lawn. Breath
of the garden, my father's work always,
this wide porch, close as she got to it.
I let my sternum rise and fall,
        rise and fall for her

      rising and falling. Once, profusion in the far beds:
yellow, orange, red tomatoes, baby pear
and little plum, their unique musk. All
those firefly summers when we'd rush to eat
as much as we could hold
        direct from the vine.

December Psalm

From the south a false warmth blows in.
Pigeons rest in their ranks on the sloped roof of Green Barn.
The arroyo willows have goldened.

Star, a slow eater, got too thin out on the hill
beneath an admonishing moon,
and has been moved indoors for healing.

> She will not tie.

We ride a strange circle:
sitting trot, posting, half-halt, halt. And walk—
repeat. Like labor-breathing.
Like the shift of seasons.

The flesh under my hand has firmed.
There are no cures but this
stability, the mountain-pony flank of her
thickening, grown warm.

> She can see in the dark.

Jasper, Alpine, Long Barn:
I love the names of paddocks—here's ramshackle blue
Bittersweet, where only Sunshine, thirty-three
and limping, will share the evening hay.

Hares poise and scatter. Sudden deer
forking their wide ears into the dusk,
pause. For the space of an *Ave*

> I can rejoice.

Our Fragile House,
Filling with Your Names

Quinces

Nearby, the water blue, and on it a white pelican swims
fishing Charleston Slough. Does that connect to the bay?

My friend is impatient because I haven't read today's *Times*
naming the Nobel Prize writer: "That really is not nice."

I do not apologize. I do not even care to
apologize. My hair is growing back. Her hair is growing back,
      thicker.

She's taken me to lunch—our salads still a streak of summer, fresh
mozzarella and tomatoes and basil, plates piled with greens—

at the shoreline. We're surviving in our different ways while the pure
pelican is dipping and dipping in his deep lagoon,

a righting instinct, and his portly self "immense," Sibley's bird guide
      said.
I tell Helen "I'm obsessed with quinces this week,"

seeing the world in a quince light. She smiles. "You remind me.
Alex loves them and when they are soft enough, eats them raw.

In Russia my mother would put them with another fruit,
blackcurrants, which will not grow here, too hot."

Quinces are in the market, fragrant, knobbed like breasts.
I take three and add two pears, following Jane Grigson's rule:

*For a rosy compote, peel, core, and boil up the panful of debris
and stir it till it turns a good, rich red.*

And cook the pieces till they soften, as I remember,
at my godmother's old house "Long Roof,"

my baby daughter asleep under the medlar tree,
the first summer just ending—her quince shape—

picked without blemish in a ruff of silver down.

Daughter

I look up and around the turn,
riding Phoebe, whose pure chestnut
is brightness tangible:

> More weight on the right seatbone, reach down
> and grab the pommel.
> Take a feel of her hair.

Did I dream this
before? This shape, its rounded joy
like a persimmon, plucked from the heavy-bearing tree.

All evening, she pursues her hay,
in that unmindful, nuzzling way of horses.
One time, November's variable star

brought me sea-colored duck eggs, a clutch.
My friend Lily believed in Jesus Christ and
13 essential vitamins and minerals:

> *Eat these*—You, by then
> swum irreversibly inside—
> *You'll be getting good news soon.*

Elegy

When the old house still belonged to us
and I could nearly touch my mother, papering the bedroom
                              as she did one year
many Sundays in her bathrobe and loafers spattered with glue
or, cooking while she sang "We Gather Together"
on Thanksgiving morning, I'd dream about the garden gate
not properly closed. I hadn't learned it never would,
needing to be hitched by wire, wound around one post.

                              *

When the pouched clouds that appeared at sunset
before rain and the last light of a fall day,
dyeing them fiery, were warming me, I knew
the old friends were dreams, and my father's gardening shed,
        sealed.
Then, when last November was cooling the ground
                              you could still say
"She died this year," those nine months, their own
small galaxy to look across and hear her voice, not quite gone—
even as doorknobs stuck and damp stains furred the wall.
Words would come from me, answering. It was certain.
It was a home, although the home I'd left, to count on.

                              *

Until, riding through this autumn on my aged mare,
I saw how sunflowers become effigies
among wild quivers of aspen gold and birch leaf.
Dismounting, running up the stirrup leathers, I felt heat
all along the inner line of my leg. Star led the way to her stall
passing the names of the dead: Jingle Bells,
                              and Sarge, and Pecos.

There was alfalfa hay, two piles, but not her partner.
Stretching out her neck, she uttered such a scream—

the jawbone, wrenched upward—
                              the world transformed to chill.

Breakfast with Persephone

We come out of the dark: our first sound, *burro* hooves
on cobbles, like a tongue clapping the roof of a mouth
(bringing firewood to sell) their light knock
before any ruction of grackles, before even the bells

which in this high Chichimecan city, they've named
for Peter, for Michael, Archangel,
and, oldest and sweetest, *La Luz*. Did you know
at the moment of birth, here, a mother is said to
                                        give light to her child?
Today on our bosky little square
my daughter and her *novio*, asleep.
I'm crouching to light the creaky gas—a match
ignites the (reed thin) candle the night-watchman
                                        keeps behind his ear—
a brass flange, opening. Holes glow blue-red.
It will take an hour for the white tiled floor to lose its cold.
Christmas. There will be a celestial event later,
new moon obscuring the sun's edge. Now we're

coming out of the dark, preceded by two cats,
the three of us, into colors of fruit—
orange and papaya, a young waiter juggling plates—
and the owner, at her papered table by the phone,

and taste of grain. Corn and oat (*avena*);
huevos mild, or less so; and one day, steamed
safely in their own sweet husks, *tamales*.
This food is not for show. It is what we yearn for

in the darkest corner of the old year, a little winter-love
like sparks flying out from a forge.

For My Daughter Seven Weeks Married

The Gilmore roses, dried to salmon, rest
in their champagne flute on my desk.

And your blue-on-cream Ketubah, rolled,
is still without a frame. What did you expect would be
the shape of remembrance?

    The Rabbi's handkerchief shook.
                                 You spiraled
    into mid-September air

    leaving just enough room for hope. Your dress
    blushed. The bridegroom spoke plain:

    As we build our life. . .
                     his scent of lavender
    became the afternoon—

    circling that seventh time, holding hands.

How long since the seminary bell struck nine? Since you were born
I've always been a light sleeper. . . If the sky were a tortoise shell,
those stars hammered on, would we feel safer?

Such a brief time beneath that wobbling tent of silk—
our fragile house, filling with your names.

Wainscott, Like As the Waves

Rose hips fatten in the hedgerow,
storing strength. I remove my shoes.

Townline Beach, the sea's turning page
after page on itself. The peeps

cry out, drilling at the clams' suckholes—
each bubble of foam is one breath

while that gull-mammocked crab has none.
Now at my feet the common stones

jewel their swath whose light only
the ocean's constant washing gives;

moving water, water moving.
Let me remember who I am,

seawind, seamind, searose, lonely
trawler on the horizon.

Let this, pure as a child's short nap,
abide: red epaulet of blackbird.

Tatters of Aphrodite

Tropicbirds

Fear not: after the glass-bottom boat tilted over Angel Reef
whose pale leafgreen coral has persevered two-thousand fold,

an inch per year, leaving that past, that underwater pitted life,
came the day's radiant point: Seacotton, kittenpaw-white

tail streamers were circling the cliff. Flight stopped. A mother
hitched
and wobbled on webbed toes toward her young one's hoarse
        breathing. His eye

already black, blackened more. All those long feathers crossed
behind, she
chose the right lizard-rustled path, thorned and
        awkward with heat.

                        *

She deposits one fish. The laughing gulls will never understand
a tropicbird's bill turning red, or how the hatchling on its own

cushion of air will start to soar. Another sanctuary here—
it happens daily like the nutmeg grated fresh on cold fruit punch—

when the cake-lady who has trekked her old round pans to the top
of the reserve, slices and hands you in waxed paper your wedge

unfrosted. It's the *God bless* she says unfailingly that feeds you
every time, deeper than chocolate bean or flour. More rich
        than sweet.

In Asa Wright's Garden

Now is the mangos' last bearing. The air thick with their reek,
I saw by torch and click-beetle light,
through transparent belly skin, a glass frog's coil of gut
and pulsing heart. And heard his song,
"Bottle-and-Spoon." A streaked flycatcher rested on his bough.

That night the cocoa forest took me in and rinsed me
with her rain. Such trust, allowing someone else to watch you sleep.
Even that torn hibiscus tipped
and spilled more nectar out. No clock, but we have the hours—
a firefly wavered off and on—
                              a change, a dewpoint coming in.

Think of this room: a jug of coconut water by the bed,
the lamp emitting whiffs of pitch-oil,
and a moth spreads herself on the pillow like a piece of cloth.
My hair will stay moist until dawn;
the forest, weaving her wet vine around all.

His ears like two pink blossoms, an agouti romps on the hill.
Mist pocketing Arima Valley, whose silver beak opens
this morning's sorcery of birds: White-beard,
violaceous, black-throat, tufted coquette—
are we closer to the dead and dying here?

The yellow mud stuck to our shoes.
A motmot cried, "Snake, Snake."
We sat down on flat rocks near the waterfall.
                              A morpho butterfly flashed
blue as a blessing through that patch of sun,
those upper wings, electric blue
                              tatters of Aphrodite.

A Cup of Cold Water

And whoever gives but a cup of cold water in my name
shall not lose his reward.
—Matthew 10:42

On Mount Saint Benedict, late afternoon
of my last day
walking with David, the gardener, who has been my guide,
coming down from the fire tower, we see
by the roadside
a blue-gray tanager
sitting
among the poinciana pods they call Woman's Tongue.
                                    The seeds
rattle—five seven-segment sections to each one.
David takes him up
spreading out the feathers' brief blue sapphire fan,

then stops. "I was going to give some sugar water."
Blood stains the base of one wing,
dark like the guava jam they make here
and label Gift of the Spirit.
                "Nothing I can do."
The bird puts its head to one side,
ear to shoulder. "When they do that. . .
                He's going to die before we get back."
Within seconds
the body
(carried on his palm) already
stiffening
"Maybe"—I need to wash my face—"at least
he knew he didn't have to die alone."
We talk about the wind.
"It whistles long, this one, with rain somewhere."

The Nesting Turtle at Matura Beach, Trinidad

She pants and the whole sea
exhales midnight ruffling a palm

Lifting her head she weeps
her eyeballs clean Still in that trance of birth

How much pound she weigh? leather and bone
Four hundred

Ashore This palazzo of dark
our kindled faces above her

She soft there I stroke her neck fold

She make plenty babies the eggs
freefalling are white they glisten

She camouflage those rear paddles
sweep coarse sand over her body

its huge flask
now pivoting through coconut velvet

to the Atlantic her jellyfish food
She is saving my life

Caroni Swamp

Here the mangrove roots are
letting down their long, jointed fingers

into salted water that is mostly mud
at this low tide. But it is rising.

Our wooden flat-bottom boat puts out
toward sunset, passing others—one named

Mighty Gideon—while the mullet,
honeycreepers and the dark tree crabs

prepare for night. A boa gathers in his knot
overhead. We are waiting, jostled in,

when the engine stops: The first ibis,
flying in their scarlet line,

arriving, a southwest light through their wings.
The mangrove island, a green hill

as these early ones, settling to roost,
fan open the red tulips of their bodies.

Dark in an hour, and all—
perhaps twenty-five hundred—will be here.

And now they flow by six, by ten, by dozens,
the land becoming one red cloud.

No other obligation than
to wonder at their color, and their trust

of home. The boatman gives a warning, swerves
the bow around. Looking back I know

in this one brief equatorial dusk,
the last crimsoned few

approaching—it is the heart's
completion, that long glide of them, coming in.

Now spring is reaching toward you again

a friend writes.
Wrapping our window moon-wise
the wisteria vine reopens this morning. Small heaven:
a cat athwart our two bodies,
her lyrical spine
        and the hum
of that steady engine, purred inside me
returned from traveling—having hung
by tedious winter threads.

Odd intimacy has followed me
        all my life.
At the Feast of the Meeting, a monk's touch
blessed my forehead:
Now let thy servant depart in peace.
Honey and crumb.

"I hope this is a happier year for you."
Out of the green trough, the chute of our creek
drains toward summer.
Light moves through the garden's violet blue
close cascades of blossom,
sweet water in the pipeline.
        Our copper beech
holds his dark throat against the stream
like a purple bird.

I Call Her My Jungle Gardenia

Perseid

In memory of Gopal Varadhan

January 3, 1969–September 11, 2001

You did not decide to leave us
for some star strummed hammock, tonight's thick blue
towelling
quietude.

No.
Grinning with your whole body
you'd have kept to your boat.
One more rebellion perhaps? and

what is not over: your brother
and your parents sleep. The Milky Way
a fine talc
pulses

above the fleshed field, this
tasseling
Algonquin corn. Like a chalk streak, a smooch mark—
your flighting

signs the damson plum air
of summer, our first
without.
My wooden chair has dampened with dew.

Hydrangeas

Dusk falls on Lafayette Street and this loft.
An album tells the lives of two
brothers, one of whom I'll never meet.

Ceremonies, threading their summers: the one-year
hair, shaved. Later, four legs poking from gold
cloth, where they were taught the secrets of men.

The younger one has come home after work—
roasted peppers glisten in their oil—
and inhales, "You smell just like my grandmother."

Who else do I have to give him but you
my daughter, those fair pigtails, silked with
coconut? Who else does his mother have,

gliding in, her sari like burnt sugar,
to receive the diamond studs? His father's lobe,
a duskywing, is buried with the lost.

Next morning, you poise the watering can
high over window-boxes while I crush
eggshells into unaccustomed soil. Magpie,

body of my body, your scissors trimmed
the evergreen; now with a spoon, tamp in new
plantlets. This doomed shock of blue, blossoming.

I Call Her My Jungle Gardenia

This hour turns in its socket, like a hip
inward, from the pier at Montauk where
                    the fat fish revel.
"Go," said the sea's cold salt wrist, "Leave this
snowed dune, and be with your living."

                  A Hindu chime sounds
saffron, and ruby. The bride's white satin taper
lights the small chapel. The groom
and she together honor the dead
(Lincoln's darkened face, in oils of all sorrow),

and make their vow.
And all the white tulips bend and extend their necks,
                as swans might,
bearing witness. Forty others.
An old bell, above, begins pealing.

Hope is an azured tie. Wainscott Hollow Road, the threshold—
When the husband's strong-suited forearms fetch her up
              and he steps them across
I can sense no lacking here: the bridal snowy swoop
of her train, her lilies, her tattoos.

To a Deer in the Forest

Life in being,
undergrowth and overgrowth
                    enfolding
your mounded knee and elbow—
Veins of branches
                    loop the wild and shaped

terrain you sleep in
and will grow to fill.

Now the young doves of April
are flying
                    through this month of my
                                        knowing.
They are the color of air and sky.
          I want flowers now,
long budded stems of gladiolas

to lay beside you
in this half-light.

Just below my diaphragm
                              a pond exists
where minnows search and swim:
          one sunlight quiver
                    at the breast-bone now
                                        and then
          is how I take you in.

The way trees fringe
a space for dreaming
                         animals—
and the body, forming—
great laws of charity protect

your secret stretch of road.
Child of my second child.

Knitting

Her belly rounds under the flowered silk.
She is becoming tomorrow's transit of Venus.
In the humid New York dusk, 19 weeks, "Mom, I just
                                        popped out."
One more dance by the wedding cake: two photos
of my mother—her blue eyes, her dress, blue—frame
your computer. "Do you have any brooches from Gran?"

When she phoned, late, the night after the amnio, "Mom,"
her husband having to be away, "Could you come?"
it was as if those briar years never happened.
                                        "We'll find soothing
                                            things to do."

Purl, Soho: We buy needles, teaching strands, and a book
with a boy on the cover. The man who has had no brother
since that September day, will have a son.
        "Go under the fence,
            lasso the sheep,
            pull him under the fence
and move the stitch." Two ladies, one on either side
(with their milky cat) explain purling: small bumps,
like a brook rushing
                    over stones.
Toots and the Maytals fill the loft. *It is no wonder. . .*
"Will you meet me at the doctor? We'll hear the heart."
Folded, creased, I keep in my notebook
                        the map she drew.

Fish Hook of Summer Stars

Vespers for Phoebe

Before waking, my finger traces the three chevrons,
freeze-branded, which grizzled her neck: each shoulder like red oak.

Climbing the ladder of sleep, my palm grows furred,
remembering the chestnut slope—fetlock to hoof. I've let something fall,

drop away: Could a horse become bodiless as law? Or was it just
that aurora she took with her into the dark.

Old news, this was, when I heard (the way a rope-wisp scours
brisk) amid the little language of the stable

how she, not lame, running free, planted her feet and broke
a pastern bone; great or lesser. Grief takes time:

I tighten the girth two holes and lengthen the reins.
We're circling. "Do you know what a figure eight is?"

A child answers, "It's an eight—that keeps on going."
Wild and bitter, the taste of radish leaps in my throat.

The hillside's succulent—blue sheen on blackbird wings—
and now, their dusk-song: Phoebe gone.

Beside the hunt field, a mingled scent of grass and animal.
The hot new mustards prick at my eyelids, like small suns.

That Nickering

She talks to her mother every night, usually walking on
Guinda to the library, looking at the sky. "Mom, are you there?"

To the tangerine moon, to Leo: twin bed of memory,
ghostly green hairnet, "I'm fine really, hope you're O.K."

Now back, past the (July) Cécile Brunner rose,
afflicted, then cured. We built a wooden trellis for it to climb.

> And, once inside, her spouse—all ready after the night
> medicine. Having lost so much, his driving taken,

> he's steering them and, finding her, reeling them in.
> *We thank you Lord for the many blessings of this day*

> lifting up his arm. She slides her head to the T-shirted chest,
> six weeks since *There is a pain at the apex of my right lung*
> woke her.

She rides every Saturday, not unlike the Galway wife who said Amen
and fled to tell the King her dreams. A field of raspberries.

"What's Montana like?" Fat and sweet, and puts her head down
when she canters. A nervous hare scurries over Webb Road.

Dusk settling on the ranch like a river, the chestnut mare
neighs softly. Food, and release. Fish hook of summer stars.

Elements of January

I.

A light came on in the gray goose-travelled dusk You went in
and sitting at the low table's ragged edge you ate
what the old woman brought Oatcakes and Stilton cheese that
      smelled of roots
from the same dairy that had been her grandfather's in the war
when you were just born *We never starved in the country* she said
That night the radiator failed and the high-ceilinged room
became a winter barn You remembered one scene from the Gallery
      hard ice
with children skating and in the foreground a man killing a pig
This was before your journey before the train set you down
on Darsham station in a fit of sleet Then over your pajamas
      drawing up
the long black woolen skirt around the collarbone you slept

II.

All night an east wind shook the reed beds like so much chaff
then it turned You woke to doves pecking the half-iced bird bath
and a thrush sang in the lane Just a twicer old Suffolk
for this two-faced month spinning its ribs in the cold You fed
the wood fire while the old woman put your knitting right
rewound the yarn began another ball weaving in the tail
Forgive me it's very basic handing back the soft blue scarf
for your new grandson *You're almost ready to cast off*
she said Outside the estuary had been weeping for its own ebb
*My prayer these days is Strengthen me Lord a little that I may go on
a bit longer* Eighty-eight this winter the first time she
didn't make her Seville marmalade Thick peel and not too sweet
gave all the jars away Meanwhile you heard dropping down
inside the stove the white-hot ends of logs their embering sound

III.

What sign were you looking for walking out of season to the sea
its raw scent the planet's blood or that singular dark cloud
funneled downward to the tide-line or back uphill the rain nested in
        your hair
at the old woman's house your godmother's where they found a
        cross dug
deep into the roof-beam four centuries ago to keep the witches out
Later you would dream about the tree next door gouged by a kick
out of nowhere came two men and did the mending from its own
        bark
Before you went to bed the elders' voices reminisced of wartime
rationing an egg a week no clothes to buy but Spring the trees in
        lace
the way a wedding dress got sewn from butter muslin
God loves a cheerful giver How long will anyone remember this

60

IV.

On the last morning you filled your cup from the thick white
      Staffordshire pot
and stepping through the French window took your tea outside
      drinking in
the bright weather while two blue-tits in all a mere fistful of bird
splashed in yesterday's puddle They flew up and balanced on the
      gutter
pushing their jonquil bellies closer to the sun In that whole week
      there was no
one moment when the past always speaking here from the old walls
      with their rounded flints
glazed by rain ceased to insist or the future's what-ifs circling like
      swallows to hover
Rather one long afternoon you knew something shifted underneath
      After the leek soup
and summer pudding red currant cherry raspberry pressed down
with a plate in the bread-lined basin till the crumbs and fruit
      dissolved into each other
tasting of the warm months the old woman and yourself seated by
      the hearth
retracing half a life swept backward to the solitary Mother Julian
      who saw God
He showed me a small thing in the palm of his hand no bigger
      than a hazelnut
It is all that is made Nearby the brewery horses Suffolk Punches
      scraped huge hooves
in their stall Steadying herself your godmother got up and walked
      with you
her hand on your crooked elbow not otherwise touching Mill Lane
      and Woodley Yard
watching them muzzle-deep in hay then homeward through the
      fine January mist

Detail, Snow in the Countryside

Two forces: storm, and the body's bent
angling into it
      Black swirl cloak and cream felt hat.
Flakes like white chrysanthemum petals
falling everywhere. Sekka called this
      Worlds of Things—the knee's
      swelling forward—the walking-stick—the brim, pulled
down—
and it would be unwise to give the wind
      some human name, ill-will or rage,
when two bare legs stump through a rivered drift.
It is age; this is the work of winter.

For Someone Lost

The blanket that used to cover us both
goes twice around me now

And this morning's fog baffles your voice
I've had to let go.

Live strong. Dangerous, giving power to that
yellow plastic bracelet. Stay strong.

Today I find an envelope,
penciled in your mother's firm hand, "First tooth.

Out, October 22, 1938." A splinter
from what would become your tall frame.

I've burned white sage in every corner.
Webs chevron the roof line.

Motet for the Guttering World

Wintertide Let this burning year slip
into a cruising of white pelicans
at wetlands' edge who herd the smaller fish
toward shallow waters I take a new a route
Here the invading fennel has been cleared away
and from a sweeping branch the sparrows map
their morning Sometimes when the long marsh wind
has died a burrowing owl will come to stand
beside that stone which looks a little like an owl
Unroiled in daylight Then the smoke of him
alighting makes me warm as wool
Let our bodies heal their great fatigues
like wet black coats outworn Let all the small wounds go
From this shore a flock of seaducks has swum
out of the floodgate Tiny golden-eyes

Nocturnal, 12 Adar

For Sylvia, whose yahrzeit this is:
Take the snapped tulips, wages of the storm,
bring Apricot Beauty, warm and inside, whose
shadow the candle's sphere of influence makes long.

These hours when bats arise (black pepper flakes)
and flow above the dirtied river,
the moon's a thinned disc,
small change in the night king's pocket.

Twenty-six hours, the flame quavers in its blue tin.
You carried me inside. The hours are rain,
the hours are rain. You who have no hours became the tulips'
shadow fluted on the blue bedroom wall.

Stake

This Saturday in August, mission figs
ripen above our redwood fence.

What no one wants to do—
glove-handed, tie a knot,
having knelt in the scent of mold to prop
deep purple heliotrope against the wind.

I pour iced tea, and call my daughter
whose voice is low
whose husband golfs among former potato fields
whose baby boy naps.

Is it hot there? When he wakes up
she'll feed him and take him outside in the shade.

Nine months, and firmly planted
beneath those beeches I've seen once,

he loves to sit and look up at the trees.

Between his breath and the wind that quickens
those copper leaves—is where I am.

Memory of Stanley Kunitz, Northampton

Baskin's owl stood sentry
in the swamping heat.

The veined elegance of the very old,
and your peony-red plaid shirt

as you took questions—"We are all
living and dying at the same moment"—

The stooped comma
of your shoulders, from fifty years'

toiling in the garden—that long
poem, never finished—

Sliding over themselves, your words
like waves of the sea,

pelagic—"What news of the great
spiral nebula in Andromeda?"—

come back to me. One bite of wild radish:
What news of Creation?

"Touch it anywhere,
and the whole web shudders."

Yes; true; on that day we were
drawn to your dying,

and this Monday in Spring, the day
of your death pronounced, we ache.

Epilogue

In This at Last May Sun, the House

Passing from you, what life was that, what lives
whose bare feet raced over the sloped oak floor?
Tilted, the earth's unstable near the creek—
our neighbor wildness, rushing off to keep
her covenant with the godwitted tide—
to pluck the salted worm or perfect snail.
You've begun leaving. The bead board, the plain
brass lock and tray ceilings not calling out,
Stay. Stay. There's no telling how lovers come
undone. Step now into this at last May
room and taste its particular sourgrass,
reckoning every element of white
pear blossom. Nothing will, they will not last
more than an instant, knowing this: here, home.

Notes

On Chesterman Beach: *Oolichan*: (fr. Chinook), also called candlefish, is a herring-like fish native to the Pacific Northwest and British Columbia, renowned as a source of food and especially, due to its high oil content, light. "So oily that when dried it may be used as a candle by drawing a wick through it" (*Webster's Dictionary*, 2nd ed., unabridged).

Light Thickens: The title is from Shakespeare's *Macbeth*, III, iii, 51.

Light Thickens: *Coyote*: a slang term for a person who smuggles illegal immigrants over the border from Mexico to the United States.

Grout: "Who telleth. . . their names." Cf. Psalm 147: 1.4.

Crazy Walk: Parts I & II "and in the evening. . . shall prosper this or that." Cf. Ecclesiastes 11:6.

And the Crow Makes Wing to the Rooky Wood: The title is from Shakespeare's *Macbeth*, III, iii, 51.

Wings of Moss: (l.1) I am indebted to Frederico Garca Lorca's "Gacela del Niño Muerto": "Los muertos llevan alas de musgo."

Ballymaloe, This Time of Year: Italicized line is from G. B. Shaw's *Major Barbara*.

Ladder to My Room: Stanza 6: "The Amherst poet rhymed. . ." Cf. Emily Dickinson, "The Bustle in a House."

Quinces: "Jane Grigson's rule. . ." Cf. her *Fruit Book*, Penguin Cookery Library, 1982.

Breakfast with Persephone: 'in the darkest corner. . .' derives from Ben Jonson's jotted reflection, "What a deale of cold

busines doth a man. . ." in his commonplace book, *Timber:
or, Discoveries.*

'Now Spring is Reaching Toward You Again': "Now let thy
servant. . ." Cf. Luke 2:29.

Hydrangeas: Stanza 2, these lines allude to the Brahmin
Hindu Sacred Thread ceremony for boys, a coming-of-age
rite. Duskywing (n.) for Propertius Duskywing, a dark-hued
butterfly.

To a Deer in the Forest: The title refers to the painting *Deer
in the Forest* by Franz Marc, one of the group of artists
known as the Blue Rider (Städtische Galerie im Lenbachhaus,
Munich).

Knitting: The phrases, "One more dance. . ." and "It is no
wonder," are from the reggae song "Sweet & Dandy" by
Toots and the Maytals (1985).

That Nickering: "Galway. . . Amen" alludes to the song
"[from] Galway to Graceland" by Richard Thompson.

Elements of January: In Section 3, the godmother is referring
to 2 Corinthians 9:6-7: "Consider this: whoever sows sparing-
ly will also reap sparingly, and whoever sows bountifully will
also reap bountifully. Each must do as already determined,
without sadness or compulsion, for God loves a cheerful
giver."

For Someone Lost: That yellow plastic bracelet: a silicone
wristband launched in May of 2004 as a fund-raising item for
the Lance Armstrong Foundation, founded by cyclist and can-
cer survivor Lance Armstrong.

Detail, Snow in the Countryside: Detail, etc., from Kamisaka
Sekka's woodblock series, *Momoyogusa I* (1909),
Rijksmuseum, Amsterdam.

Motet for the Guttering World: Gutter (v.) To melt away through the side of the hollow formed by a burning wick. Used of a candle.

Nocturnal, 12 Adar: Adar is the sixth month of the year in the Jewish calendar, corresponding to parts of February and March. Yahrzeit is the commemoration of a Jewish person's death by a mourner; the date is calculated according to the Hebrew calendar. One expression of the Yahrzeit is lighting a special memorial candle to burn 24 hours.

Memory of Stanley Kunitz, Northampton: This poem arose from Kunitz's reading for the Smith College Poetry Center in April, 2002. He died in May, 2006 at the age of 100. The line "What news of the great spiral nebula in Andromeda?" is quoted from Kunitz's "Halley's Comet." ". . .drawn to your dying" derives from a line in Kunitz's "The Wellfleet Whale": "What drew us to your dying?"

Further Acknowledgments

No strict form can express how much I owe the poetry communities to which I belong. You have listened to my work—often many times—and heard its voice, even when I thought it lost. And we've had so much fun! I'm grateful to:

Waverley Writers, my poetry home: Squaw Valley Community of Writers, particularly Lucile Clifton, Robert Hass, Galway Kinnell, Sharon Olds, Dean Young and Brett Hall Jones. You helped me write what had been unwriteable before; Thursday Night Poets—the focal point of my week—especially Chris and David Cummings, Shirley Gaines, Meredith Ittner, Muriel Karr, and Eve Sutton; Palo Alto's Waverley Writers, my poetry home; and Squaw Valley Community of Writers, particularly Lucile Clifton, Robert Haas, Galway Kinnell, Sharon Olds, Dean Young and Brett Hall Jones. All of you have helped me write what had been unwriteable before.

For their patience with my pragmatic and technical failings I'm indebted to Ken Easterby and Debby Brown, Keith Bartel and Carole Loza.

For your steadfast friendship—Sonja and Ivan Levinger, Bambi and Michael Good, Nancy Flowers, Patricia Evans Weiss, *gracias por todo.*

Also, thank you, Stanford Community Boot Camp, 6 a.m!

Without my family, this book could not have happened. Loving thanks to Susan Finer and Ellen Toker, my sisters; Kate Freeman and Maggie Varadhan, my daughters, and to Gavin Varadhan, my grandson.

To the editors at Ashland Poetry Press: I appreciate your kind and straightforward attention, and well-honed skills.

For truly inspiring me, I thank Richard Chapman, Edward (Pete) Warren, S.J. and Mary (Peggy) Purves, of blessed memory.

The Robert McGovern Publication Prize is awarded to poets over 40 years of age who have published no more than one book. The prize is established in memory of Robert McGovern, poet, professor, co-founder of the Ashland Poetry Press, and long-time chair of the English Department at Ashland University. Manuscripts are submitted by nomination. The McGovern nominating panel currently consists of Annie Finch, Carolyn Forché, Alice Fulton, Eamon Grennan, William Heyen, Andrew Hudgins, Richard Jackson, John Kinsella, Gerry LaFemina, Philip Levine, Robert Phillips, Vern Rutsala, Enid Shomer, and Gregory Wolfe. Ashland Poetry Press Editors also occasionally make an "Editor's Choice" selection for the McGovern series, outside of the regular nomination process.

Winners of the McGovern Prize are as follows:

Elizabeth Biller Chapman, for *Light Thickens* (nominated by
    Enid Shomer)
Michael Miller, for *The Joyful Dark* (Editor's Choice, selected
    by Stephen Haven)
Maria Terrone, for *A Secret Room in Fall* (nominated by
    Gerry LaFemina)
Nathalie Anderson, for *Crawlers* (nominated by
    Eamon Grennan)
A.V. Christie, for *The Housing* (nominated by
    Eamon Grennan)
Jerry Harp, for *Gatherings* (nominated by John Kinsella)